Tycho Brahe

Astronomer

GREAT MINDS OF SCIENCE

Tycho Brahe

Astronomer

Mary Gow

 Enslow Publishers, Inc.

40 Industrial Road	PO Box 38
Box 398	Aldershot
Berkeley Heights, NJ 07922	Hants GU12 6BP
USA	UK

http://www.enslow.com

To Steve

Library of Congress Cataloging-in-Publication Data

Gow, Mary.
    Tycho Brahe : astronomer / by Mary Gow.
      p. cm. — (Great minds of science)
    Includes bibliographical references and index.
    Summary: Presents the life and work of the famous sixteenth-century
Danish astronomer.
    ISBN 0-7660-1757-5
    1. Brahe, Tycho, 1546-1601—Juvenile literature. 2. Astronomers—
Denmark—Biography—Juvenile literature. [1. Brahe, Tycho, 1546-1601. 2.
Astronomers.] I. Title. II. Series.
    QB36.B8 G69 2002
    520'.92—dc21

                    2001003269

Printed in the United States of America

10 9 8 7 6 5 4 3 2 1

To Our Readers:
We have done our best to make sure all Internet addresses in this book
were active and appropriate when we went to press. However, the
author and the publisher have no control over and assume no liabili-
ty for the material available on those Internet sites or on other Web
sites they may link to. Any comments or suggestions can be sent by
e-mail to comments@enslow.com or to the address on the back cover.

Illustration Credits: Det Nationalhistoriske Museum på Frederiks-
borg, Hillerød, pp. 10, 48, 68, 89; Enslow Publishers, Inc., pp. 19, 108;
ROSAT Mission <http:il~~w.xray.mpe.mpg.de/> and Max-Planck-
Institut fur extraterrestrische Physik <http:1/www.mpe.mpg.de/>,
p. 43; The History of Science Collections, University of Oklahoma, pp.
14, 28, 32, 40, 50, 57, 62, 65, 73, 78, 81, 87, 96, 98, 100; Viveca
Ohlsson, Landskrona Museum, pp. 22, 104.

Cover Illustration: NASA (background); History of Science
Collections, University of Oklahoma (inset).

Contents

The Castle of
the Heavens

AN EXTRAORDINARY CASTLE ONCE stood on the little Danish island of Hven. A gold weather vane of Pegasus, the winged horse, twirled on the castle's highest spire. Astronomical instruments stood on its balconies. In the castle library sat a huge brass globe with 1,000 stars drawn on it. The building hummed with voices speaking Latin, Danish, Dutch, and German. The castle was named Uraniborg, Castle of the Heavens.

Tycho Brahe, the master of Uraniborg, was as extraordinary as his castle. He wore a ruffled collar, white lace cuffs, and a black cloak. A small gold elephant hung on a gold chain around his neck. The elephant was a gift from the king of Denmark. Brahe had hazel eyes, reddish blonde hair, and a long flowing mustache. His face was attractive but unusual. Instead of flesh, his nose was made of metal.

Tycho Brahe was the world's most famous observational astronomer.[1] Uraniborg was the world's first modern observatory.

Observational astronomy is the study of the positions and movements of celestial bodies. Observational astronomers watch the stars, planets, sun, moon, and comets. They study objects they see in the sky. (Other kinds of astronomers study the origins of the universe, its chemistry, and the laws of physics that affect it.) An observatory is a building designed and equipped to study the heavens.

Tycho Brahe was born in 1546. He died in 1601, eight years before the telescope was invented. Even without a telescope, Tycho Brahe and his observations shaped modern astronomy.

Tycho's goal was to "lay the foundations of and develop a renewed Astronomy."[2] He wanted to figure out how celestial bodies moved—to know when they would be in different positions in the sky. Tycho believed that if he had accurate observations showing where the sun, moon, planets, and stars were on many dates and at many times, he would recognize patterns in their movement. The observations needed to be accurate to be truly useful. Tycho spent thirty-five years recording these observations.

Tycho's observations were the most accurate ones in the world at his time and for many years. Their accuracy helped him make important discoveries about the universe. They helped him develop theories about the movement of the moon and the planets. His observations also provided crucial information that allowed another astronomer, Johannes Kepler, to make a revolutionary discovery about the shape of planetary orbits. Because of Tycho Brahe, people began to see Earth and the universe in a new way.

Heinrich Hansen's 1862 painting of Uraniborg, based on sixteenth century woodcuts. Pegasus, the winged horse, is atop the center spire.

In sixteenth-century Europe, most people believed that Earth stood still at the center of the universe. They thought that the moon, planets, the sun, and stars traveled around Earth in crystal spheres. Tycho also believed that Earth stood at the center of the universe. He suspected, however, that the universe was not so simply explained.

From the time Tycho was fourteen years old, he wanted to understand the heavens. He bought astronomy books and star charts. When he was sent to school to study law, he secretly spent nights observing the stars. When he was seventeen, he observed a conjunction of the planets Jupiter and Saturn. A conjunction is when two celestial objects appear to line up in the sky. Charts and formulas that calculated celestial movements existed, but Tycho's observation of the conjunction showed him that those charts were flawed. The conjunction did not occur when it was predicted. That was when he decided that new observations were needed to decode the movements of the heavens.[3]

To understand some of Tycho's questions about the universe, imagine that you are outside on a clear winter evening. You look at the sky. One star is brighter than all the others. It is in the west. It does not twinkle like other stars; it glows with a steady light. For several evenings you go out and look at your star. Each night it sets earlier. You realize that each night it is in a different place relative to the stars around it. Your star is slowly shifting to the west.

For several months you do not look for your star. When you go out to look again, it is not there. You search the sky. No star is as bright as the one you saw in the winter. Early the next morning, before the sun is up, you go outside. There, in the east, is your star, the brightest one in the sky. You watch it for several days. It gradually shifts east against the background stars.

Your star is the planet Venus. Venus is the third brightest celestial object. Only the sun and moon are brighter. Venus, you observe, has wandered from a position behind the sun in the western sky to a position ahead of the sun in the eastern sky.

Besides that, it has changed its position relative to the background stars. First it wandered toward the west. Then it shifted to the east.

The word *planet* comes from the Greek word meaning "wanderer." The Greeks named the planets wanderers because of their apparent movement in the sky. Tycho wanted to understand the planets' wandering. He believed with enough observations, he could figure out the paths of these wanderers.

In 1576, King Frederick II of Denmark gave the island of Hven to Tycho Brahe. Tycho built Uraniborg, his Castle of the Heavens, there. For many years, he made observations from his magnificent castle observatory. Students and assistants came to Uraniborg to work with him and help him observe.

Tycho built Uraniborg to be an almost magical place, dedicated to the pursuit of knowledge. Beauty, he believed, inspired great thoughts. The castle's graceful spires reached toward the sky. Fragrant flowers and exotic fruit trees filled its gardens. A bronze fountain inside

Portrait of Tycho Brahe from Instaurate Mechanica, *surrounded by the coats of arms of his sixteen great-great grandparents, all of noble families. Note the gold elephant from the king on his chain.*

the castle cast streams of water into the air. Splendid paintings of philosophers and astronomers decorated its rooms.

Exquisite and gracious, Uraniborg was also a well-planned research center. Its twin towers were large observatories facing north and south. Smaller observatories flanked the towers. Three thousand books and Tycho's enormous celestial globe sat in Uraniborg's library. Installed in a spacious southwest room was the mural quadrant, a handsome and precise instrument used to measure the altitude of celestial bodies.

Tycho spent almost forty years observing the heavens. He watched a new, very bright star make its explosive appearance and slowly fade away. This is what we now call a supernova. He observed seven comets. He measured and plotted the positions of over a thousand stars. He studied the movements of the five planets other than Earth that are visible to the naked eye: Mercury, Venus, Mars, Jupiter, and Saturn. Tycho developed theories to explain the heavens. He built the most precise astronomical instruments of his time, and he wrote books explaining his research and discoveries.

Tycho Brahe's research expanded humankind's understanding of Earth's place in the universe. Tycho was an astronomer of extraordinary ability and vision. He renewed astronomy and laid the foundation for new discoveries and knowledge.

Noble Beginnings

TYCHO BRAHE WAS BORN ON DECEMBER 14, 1546, at his family's home in Knutstrup. Knutstrup was then in Denmark but is now in Sweden. He probably wiggled his toes and uttered his first little cries in the manor house there. Tycho's parents built a handsome brick castle at Knutstrup, but it wasn't finished until Tycho was almost five.[1]

Tycho's parents, Otto Brahe and Beate Bille, were used to living in castles. The Brahes and the Billes were two of the most powerful noble families in Denmark. Brahes and Billes owned land and forests and farms. They owned lovely homes in Copenhagen and other Danish cities.

In the 1500s, the king of Denmark often gave lands, called fiefs, to his noblemen. The noblemen managed their fiefs according to the laws of Denmark. They collected rent and taxes from the people who lived on their lands. On some fiefs, instead of paying rent, the people owed work to the nobleman. The Brahes and the Billes controlled many fiefs.

For generations, Brahe and Bille men served Danish kings. They sat on the Rigsraad, the most important council in Denmark. The Rigsraad advised the king about war and peace and the country's business. When there were wars, Brahe and Bille men put on their armor, carried swords, and led armies to fight for Denmark.

Brahe and Bille women married noblemen and had noble children. They usually had many children. Because of disease and lack of medical knowledge, one quarter of noble children did not live to adulthood. (Only half of the babies born to poor commoners lived to their tenth birthdays.)[2]

When Otto Brahe married Beate Bille in 1544, their two powerful families were joined. Their children would be born to privilege and wealth. Servants would prepare their meals and clean their rooms. As nobles, they would wear silk, linen, lace, and fur. The girls' gowns would be decorated with pearls and jewels. The boys would carry swords. They would learn to govern fiefs.

Otto Brahe and Beate Bille's first child was a daughter, Lisbeth. In December 1546, Beate gave birth to twin boys. One baby did not live long enough to be baptized and named. The other baby survived. He was named Tyge, for his Brahe grandfather. (Tyge changed his name to Tycho when he was a teenager.)

Tycho did not find out about his twin until he was about twenty-five years old. When he learned about his brother, he wrote a Latin poem and dedicated it to him. In the poem, Tycho wondered which twin had a happier fate.[3]

This map shows the boundaries of European nations as they existed in the time of Tycho Brahe.

Losing his twin was not the only unusual circumstance of Tycho's very young life. When Tycho was less than two years old, his uncle kidnapped him. Jørgen Brahe, Otto's older brother, "without the knowledge of my parents [took] me away with him while I was in my earliest youth," wrote Tycho. "He supported me generously during his lifetime."[4]

Jørgen and his wife, Inger Oxe, did not have any children of their own. There may have been an arrangement that Otto and Beate would let them raise one of their sons. Jørgen, however, did not wait.[5] At first, Tycho's parents were angry that Jørgen had taken their baby. Later, they accepted it. Otto and Beate eventually had twelve children; eight of them survived childhood. Jørgen and Inger only had Tycho.

We do not have many details about Tycho's childhood. We do know that it was different with Inger Oxe and Jørgen Brahe than it would have been with his biological parents. "My father, Otto Brahe . . . was not particularly anxious that his five sons, of whom I am the eldest, should learn Latin," wrote Tycho.[6]

Latin, in Tycho Brahe's time, was the language of education. University-educated young men read, wrote, and spoke Latin. Tycho's schooling started when he was seven years old. He learned Latin grammar. His early studies probably also included Lutheran religion, ancient Greek language, and mathematics.

Many young noblemen were not educated in universities. Instead, they went to the castles of other noblemen, often in Germany. There they perfected their horsemanship, sword-fighting skills, and court manners. They learned to be military leaders. This was the life that Otto Brahe arranged for his other sons.[7]

Tycho did not follow the traditional Brahe training. His stepmother, Inger Oxe, was probably the reason. Unlike the Brahes, the Oxes had a long tradition of education. They studied in universities. They were statesmen instead of military leaders. Inger's brother,

Brahe family portrait in Kagerod Church. Otto Brahe and Beate Bille in center. Behind Otto are his sons Tycho, Steen, Knud, Axel, and Jorgen. Behind Beate are Lisbet, Maren, Margrete, Kirsten, and Sophie. Notice that Maren, who died as a baby, and Kirsten, who died when she was around thirteen, are represented at their young ages.

Peder Oxe, held one of the highest positions in Danish government.

When Tycho was twelve, he went to the University of Copenhagen. He read poems, plays, and history written in Latin. He studied public speaking, arithmetic, geometry, astronomy, and music. Many university students changed their names to their Latin form. This is when Tyge became Tycho.

Tycho may have seen a partial eclipse of the sun in August 1560. A solar eclipse occurs when the moon passes between Earth and the sun. In a total eclipse, the moon completely covers the sun. The sky becomes dark. In Copenhagen in 1560, the moon only partly covered the sun. Unless the sky was clear, the eclipse would not have been obvious. Tycho heard about the eclipse even if he did not see it. He wrote how thrilling it was that people could predict the movements of the heavens.[8] Soon afterward Tycho bought his first astronomy book. He wrote his name in it. This book is now in the Danish National Museum.

Tycho's fascination with the heavens had started.

When Tycho was fifteen, Jørgen sent him to law school in Germany. Jørgen also sent a tutor named Anders Vedel along. Vedel was nineteen years old. He was studying history. He was supposed to arrange Tycho's classes, manage his money, and make sure that Tycho studied law. Tycho had other ideas.

"In Leipzig," Tycho explains, "I began to study Astronomy more and more. This I did in spite of the fact my governor (Vedel), who pleading the wishes of my parents wanted me to study law." He continued, "I bought the astronomical books secretly, and read them in secret in order that the governor should not become aware of it."[9]

Tycho bought himself a little celestial globe, a sphere with stars and constellations drawn on it. He studied his globe. Night after night he gazed at the stars.

"By and by," he wrote, " I got accustomed to distinguishing the constellations of the sky, and in the course of a month I learnt to know them all."[10]

On August 24, 1563, a celestial event started Tycho on his path to becoming an astronomer.

Jupiter, Saturn and Tycho's Nose

TO UNDERSTAND THE IMPORTANCE OF August 24, 1563, to Tycho, we need to understand his view of Earth and the heavens. Europeans in the 1500s, including Tycho, believed that Earth was at the center of the universe. They knew that Earth was a sphere. Columbus had discovered America in 1492. Ferdinand Magellan's ship circled the world in 1522.

Even before Columbus's voyage, most people knew that Earth was round. Aristotle, one of the most famous of the ancient Greek philosophers, lived during the fourth century B.C. Aristotle knew that Earth was a sphere.

Aristotle believed that Earth was at the center of the universe. He thought that the heavenly bodies sat in crystal spheres that rotated around Earth. The moon was in the smallest sphere, the one closest to Earth. It was followed by spheres holding Mercury, Venus, Mars, Jupiter, Saturn, and the sun. These were the wanderers. Each of these celestial bodies had its own pattern of movement. The fixed stars all appeared to move together. Aristotle explained that they were all on the largest rotating sphere. For many centuries, most Europeans believed Aristotle's explanation.

Five hundred years after Aristotle, a Greek mathematician named Ptolemy, who was living in Egypt, made some changes to the model. He wrote a very detailed book, the *Almagest*, around 150 A.D. Almagest means "the greatest" in Arabic, and it was the greatest astronomy book for many centuries.

Ptolemy believed that the movements of the heavens, including the planets, could be explained in mathematical terms. His book provided tables and formulas to calculate the positions of celestial objects.

Ptolemy thought that the planets moved in small circles on their crystal spheres. These small circles were called epicycles. Like Aristotle, he believed the unmoving Earth sat at the center of the universe.

Ptolemy's model of the universe became accepted by the Christian religion. The Bible says the sun rose and set. Many people believed that the Bible meant that Earth was unmoving. Ptolemy's explanation agreed with this belief.

Most people in Tycho Brahe's time, including Tycho, believed in astrology. Astrology is the study of the influence of heavenly bodies on Earth. People who believe in astrology think that planets and stars can affect a person's character and fate. Some people still believe in astrological predictions called horoscopes. In Tycho's time, astrology was a serious subject. It was not considered superstition. Kings often asked astrologers for advice.

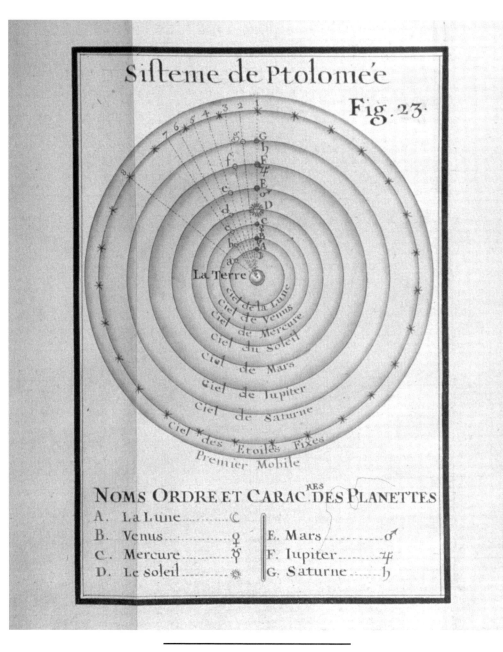

Ptolemy's model of the universe, from Traite de Sphere.

Nicolaus Copernicus, a Polish mathematician, died three years before Tycho was born. Copernicus wrote a book titled *On the Revolutions of the Celestial Spheres*. The book was published in 1543, the same year he died. In his book, Copernicus proposed that Earth and the planets circle the sun.

As Tycho studied astronomy, he learned of Copernicus's work. He admired Copernicus's mathematical skill. But Tycho still believed that Earth was at the center of the universe.

In August 1563, Tycho was in Leipzig, Germany. That month the planets Jupiter and Saturn would be in conjunction. At conjunction, one heavenly body appears to be directly above the other one. Conjunctions of Jupiter and Saturn happen every twenty years.

Tycho looked forward to the conjunction. He watched the planets move closer and closer to each other. On August 24, the conjunction occurred. Jupiter and Saturn were so near to each other that Tycho could barely measure the angle between them. The conjunction was thrilling to see, but it was troubling to Tycho. It occurred a month earlier than Ptolemy's astronomical tables predicted. Copernicus's calculations for the conjunction were incorrect, too.[1]

The conjunction of Saturn and Jupiter showed Tycho that existing information about the planets was inaccurate. He decided that new, more accurate observations were needed.

After the conjunction, Tycho started keeping an astronomical journal. He began observing often and writing down his observations in his journal. He bought an astronomical radius, an instrument used to measure the angle between celestial objects.

"When I got this radius," Tycho wrote, "I eagerly set about making stellar observations whenever I enjoyed the benefit of a clear sky, and often I stayed awake the whole night through, while my governor [Vedel] slept and knew nothing about it; for I observed the stars through a skylight and entered the observations specially in a small book, which is still in my possession."[2]

While Tycho was in Leipzig, a war started between Denmark and Sweden. Tycho was called home in May 1565. In the war, Tycho's Brahe grandparents died defending their Baahus Castle. Tycho's adoptive father, his uncle Jørgen, commanded a Danish warship. Jørgen captured the admiral of the Swedish Navy. He was a war hero.

When Tycho arrived home, Jørgen was in Copenhagen, Denmark's capital. He was organizing ships and men for battle. Late one night, Jørgen and King Frederick II fell off a bridge near the king's castle. They were soaked in the frigid seawater. The king, by some accounts, fell in first. Jørgen jumped in to save him. Neither man drowned, but Jørgen never recovered. He died a few weeks later from the effects of the chill.[3]

After Jørgen's death, Tycho remained in Denmark. He stayed at Knutstrup and spent time with his parents. He got to know his younger brothers and sisters. His older sister, Lisbeth, had died giving birth to a daughter.

In the spring Tycho Brahe returned to Germany. He moved to the city of Rostock.

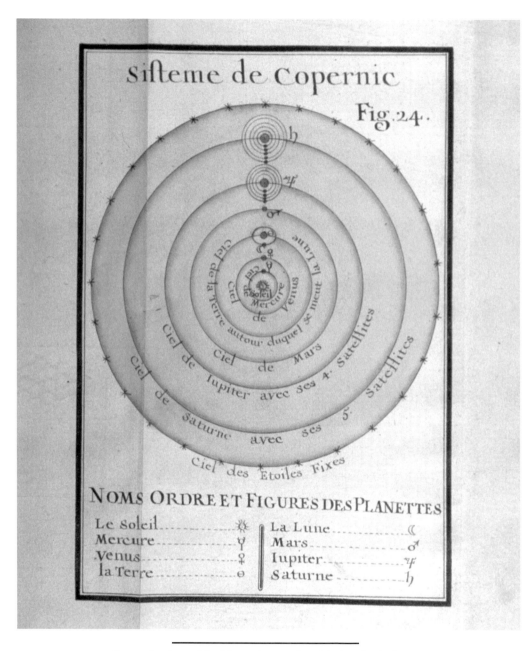

Copernicus's model of the universe, from Traite de Sphere.

Many young Danes studied there. He registered for classes at the university.

Tycho observed the stars and planets while he was in Rostock. He also studied astrology. He began to predict how celestial events might influence people's lives. An eclipse of the moon was to occur in late October. Tycho believed that it meant that the Turkish sultan, Süleyman the Magnificent, would die. Tycho was so sure of his interpretation that he wrote a poem about it. But the sultan died six weeks before the eclipse.[4] Tycho was ridiculed by the other students.

On December 10, 1566, Tycho was at an engagement party. Amid the celebrations he argued with his distant cousin, Manderup Parsberg. The dispute may have been about Tycho's prediction. Some stories say they argued over which of them was the better mathematician. After Christmas, they quarreled again.

On December 29, words turned to blows. Tycho and Parsberg met for a third time. They argued bitterly at the dinner table. Then they went outside to settle their dispute. Like other young noblemen of the time, both Tycho and Parsberg carried swords.

When the brawl was over, Tycho's face was changed. Parsberg's sword probably hit Brahe's forehead first. Then it hacked off Brahe's nose. Parsberg was not injured.

The wound in the middle of Brahe's face healed slowly. New skin had to grow around his exposed nasal opening. With the limited medicines of the time, he was at risk of getting a deadly infection.

Tycho recovered, but his nose was gone. For the rest of his life he wore a prosthesis, an artificial nose. Tycho supposedly had two artificial noses. One was made of gold and silver blended together to look like flesh. He wore that one for special occasions. Gold is heavy, though, and a heavy nose can fall off. He apparently had a lightweight nose made of copper for everyday wear.[5] He carried a jar of sticky ointment with him to fasten his nose back on whenever it jiggled loose.

Supernova!

TYCHO SPENT MOST OF THE TIME FROM 1566 through 1570 in Germany. He continued studying the heavens. A spectacular celestial event would soon make him famous.

In Germany Tycho started designing astronomical instruments. A quadrant is an instrument that can measure altitude, how high an object is above the horizon. Tycho and Paul Hainzel, a German nobleman, wanted to take very accurate measurements. They wanted to be accurate to one sixtieth of a degree, called one minute of arc. They believed a large instrument could be that precise. Tycho designed a quadrant with a nineteen-foot radius. Hainzel paid to have it built. The quadrant was made of oak with a strip of brass engraved with degrees and minutes of arc. Forty men were needed to set it up. The quadrant was quite accurate but extremely awkward to use. Because of its immense size, it was kept outdoors. It was used for about five years before a storm destroyed it.

Also in Germany, Tycho ordered a wooden globe almost six feet in diameter. He planned to show the positions of the stars on it. Years later he had it covered with polished sheets of brass. One thousand stars were precisely drawn on it. This sphere became Tycho's famous celestial globe.

In late 1570 Tycho was called back to Denmark. His father was very sick. Otto Brahe died in May 1571. His estate included 500 farms, 60 cottages, 14 mills, houses in Copenhagen, manor houses in the country, Knutstrup Castle, and more.[1] Tycho and his brother Steen inherited Knutstrup.

Tycho stayed in Denmark while Otto's estate was settled. He spent time at Knutstrup with his mother. It was at this time that he learned about his twin brother. After a few months he went to stay with his uncle, Steen Bille, who lived several miles away.

Steen Bille was educated. He loved writing poetry. He collected ancient manuscripts. He was fascinated by alchemy, an early form of chemistry. Steen encouraged Tycho's research.

On the evening of November 11, 1572, Tycho Brahe saw his second life-changing celestial event. He was walking back to Steen Bille's house for dinner. Disbelief flooded over him when he looked at the sky. A dazzling new star sparkled in the constellation Cassiopeia. Cassiopeia is the constellation that looks like the letter W. It appears in the north sky, near the North Star.

Amazed, Tycho asked his servants if they saw the star. They did. Tycho called out to some nearby peasants. They saw the star, too. Tycho did not believe his eyes.[2]

Immediately Tycho's scientific mind took over. He started measuring and observing the star. He measured its position relative to the other nine stars in the constellation Cassiopeia. He drew diagrams of Cassiopeia and the star. He wrote down the star's brightness, color, and appearance. It was as bright as Venus. It was white. It twinkled like a star instead of glowing like a planet.

Night after night, Tycho observed the new star. He observed it at early hours and at later hours. In very clear weather he could see the star during the day.[3]

Tycho took many careful measurements of the star's position. He was trying to learn how close the star was to Earth. He was looking for the star's parallax.

Parallax is the apparent movement of a close object relative to a distant object. Parallax reveals whether two objects are at the same distance from an observer or if one is nearer than the other.

Imagine that your head is Earth, your index finger is an object in space, and the knob on the door across the room from you is a star. (If you don't have a knob, any spot on the wall will work.)

Stretch your arm in front of you with your finger pointing to the knob. Close your left eye and look through your right eye. Now switch. Open your left and close your right. Relative to the background, your finger appears to have moved to the right. The apparent movement of your finger shows that your finger is nearer to you than the knob.

When you looked through your left eye, it was as though you looked out from one position on Earth. Your right eye gave you the view from another position on Earth.

Tycho was trying to see if the new star moved relative to the stars around it. If it did, then it was closer than those other stars. If it did not move, then it was as far away as the other stars.

Tycho was looking for diurnal, or daily, parallax. With Tycho's many measurements, he found no parallax for the new star.

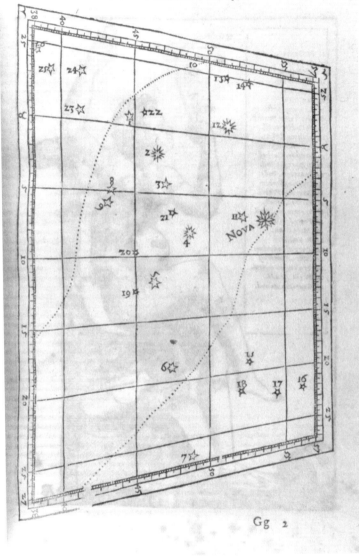

Gg 2

The new star of 1572, from Tycho's Opera Omnia, *showing the supernova, labeled "NOVA" where he observed it in the constellation Cassiopeia.*

We now know that what Tycho and thousands of other people saw from November 1572 to April 1574 was a supernova. Tycho was correct that it was a star, but it was not a new star. It was the massive explosion of a large dying star.

In Latin *nova stella* means "new star." Many years after Tycho, *nova* became the term for a type of variable star that increases in brightness. *Supernova* became the term for a specific type of spectacular stellar explosion.

Stars that become supernovas are very large. A classic supernova is called a Type I supernova. It begins as a star with at least eight times the mass of our sun. For millions of years the star burns hydrogen. Hydrogen is the lightest element.

When the star runs out of hydrogen, it starts burning other elements. It uses up its helium, then moves on. When it gets to heavier elements, the fireworks begin. The star's interior collapses. With a great explosion, the star blasts its outer layers into space. The star flashes. Atomic nuclei, X-rays, light waves, and cosmic rays explode into the universe.

Besides being a spectacular light show, other interesting things happen with supernovas. The star's core keeps collapsing. It becomes either a black hole or a neutron star. Both of these are very, very dense stars with extraordinary gravitational pull. Black holes are among the universe's most bizarre objects. They are so dense that even light cannot escape their gravity. Today, satellite photographs help scientists make many new discoveries about supernovas and black holes.

The remnant of Tycho's supernova was discovered in the 1960s by scientists at the Mount Palomar telescope. It was photographed with a telescope on board the ROSAT spacecraft. ROSAT is an international space research project. Tycho's supernova remnant is identified as SNR 1572.[4] More than 400 years after Tycho saw it, this supernova is still being studied.

Astronomers estimate that three supernovas occur each century in a galaxy the size of our Milky Way. They are seldom seen because they are hidden by galactic clouds.

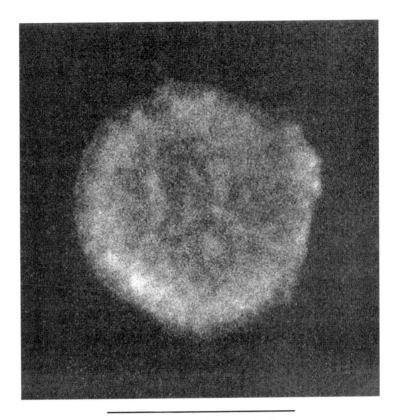

Tycho's Supernova Remnant in X-ray.

In 1987, people in the Southern Hemisphere saw a supernova in a galaxy called the Large Magellanic Cloud. It was visible without a telescope for several weeks.

Tycho observed that the new star was farther away than he could measure—probably as far away as the other stars. This view was different from the beliefs of his time. People believed that the celestial sphere never changed. Tycho's observations showed that this was not true.

In January 1573, Tycho had already been observing the star for two months. He kept his observations in a journal. The star was becoming fainter. Its color had changed to yellow.

Visiting in Copenhagen, Tycho shared his observations with his friend Johannes Pratensis. Pratensis had not noticed the star himself. He was amazed by Tycho's work. He and the king of Denmark, Frederick II, urged Tycho to publish his observations. In May 1573 Tycho published a booklet usually called by its shortened name *De stella nova* (Latin for "On the new star": Tycho wrote this book and most of his others in Latin).

Tycho's book traveled to cities and universities across Europe. Scientists and mathematicians read *De stella nova* and saw Tycho's observations. They studied his parallax calculations. They recognized Tycho's brilliance as an astronomer.

Settling Down

A YOUNG WOMAN NAMED KIRSTEN Jørgensdatter came into Tycho Brahe's life at around the same time as the supernova. Jørgensdatter was the daughter of the minister in Knutstrup.[1] They probably met while Tycho was staying with his mother. By the time *De stella nova* was published, Kirsten and Tycho were a couple. Their first daughter, Kirstine, was born that fall.

Kirsten and Tycho were together from 1573 to the end of Tycho's life. They had eight children; six lived to adulthood.

Tycho and Kirsten never formally married. The laws of Denmark in the 1500s did not allow nobles to marry commoners. Tycho Brahe was a nobleman. Kirsten Jørgensdatter was a commoner.

Danish social classes were clearly defined in Tycho's time. Class was determined by birth. Royal parents had royal children. Noble parents had noble children. Commoners had common children. Education and achievement did not change social class.

For noble families like the Brahes and the Billes, laws about class separation helped keep them wealthy. Their lands, castles, and money could only be inherited by their noble children. As long as nobles married only each other, money and land stayed in their control.

Although Tycho and Kirsten could not marry, an ancient Danish law provided another option. A common woman could be considered a nobleman's *slegfred* wife under certain conditions. The couple had to be together for at least three years. The woman had to live openly with the man, eat at his table, and carry the keys to his household. Tycho Brahe and Kirsten Jørgensdatter spent almost thirty years together. They lived and ate together. Kirsten certainly carried the household keys.[2]

As a slegfred wife, Kirsten remained a commoner. Tycho remained a noble. Their children were common, like their mother. As commoners, they could not inherit their father's name, his coat of arms, or his property.[3]

In 1574 Tycho and Kirsten moved to Copenhagen. There, their daughter, Magdalene, was born. Tycho lectured at the University of Copenhagen for several months.

The following spring Tycho went on another foreign trip. He visited universities and cities in Germany and Italy. He met astronomers, mathematicians, and philosophers. Many of them had read *De stella nova*. Tycho came home at the end of the year. He quietly started making plans to move with Kirsten to Germany.

Early on the morning of February 11, 1576, a messenger from King Frederick II arrived at the

Frederik II, King of Denmark, 1534–1588. Portrait by Hans de Knieper, painted in 1581.

Brahe castle at Knutstrup. His message was very important. He delivered it to Tycho Brahe in his bed. Frederick commanded Tycho to come see him.[4]

Tycho left immediately. He arrived at the king's hunting lodge in the evening.

Frederick knew that Tycho was famous throughout Europe. He heard that Tycho was thinking about moving. The king did not want

Denmark's gifted astronomer to live in another country.

A little island called Hven rises in the middle of Øresund ("The Sound") in Denmark. The king could see it from his castle at Elsinore. The island, the king thought, would be perfect for Tycho. (Hven at that time was in Denmark. Boundaries changed in a war in the 1600s and it became part of Sweden; it still is today.)

When Tycho arrived at the king's hunting lodge, Frederick made him an offer. He offered him Hven.

"He asked me to erect buildings on this island, and to construct instruments for astronomical investigations as well as for chemical studies," Tycho wrote of the king's offer, "and he graciously promised me that he would abundantly defray the expenses."[5]

Nine miles from the mainland, Hven was surrounded by the sea. On Hven, Tycho could observe the stars in all directions, with no mountains or buildings in the way. The island's isolation would give him privacy. He could

View of the Oresund Sound with the island of Hven, 1588. The king of Denmark's Castle of Elsinore is in the foreground. Tycho's Uraniborg is visible on Hven.

concentrate on his observations and research. On Hven, Tycho Brahe and Kirsten Jørgensdatter and their children could live together away from the social problems caused by their being in separate classes.

On February 22 Tycho visited his island. He recorded his first celestial observation on Hven: a conjunction of Mars and the moon.

Hven is a small island, about three miles long and a mile and a half wide. Like a shelf, it sits on top of cliffs and steep slopes that rise from the sound. Wild winds whip across in stormy weather.

Winter nights on Hven, as in all of Denmark, are long. In December, the sun shines barely seven hours a day. For about seventeen hours the island is in darkness.

When Frederick granted Hven to Tycho, about fifty families already lived there. Their rustic houses were clustered in the little village of Tuna. They worshiped in St. Ibbs Church, perched atop the cliffs at the island's north end. The islanders planted oats and rye in fields around the village. Cattle and horses grazed in their meadows. Pigs, ducks, and geese waddled through their farmyards and village lanes.[6]

Along with the island, Tycho got the islanders. Before Tycho, Hven was not part of an assigned fief. The islanders paid taxes to the king. They were usually left alone. Now Tycho was the lord of the island. He owned Hven. The islanders owed tax to him. They also had to work for him. Every Hven household owed Tycho two days of labor every week, from sunup to sundown, without pay.[7] Tycho's arrival was not happy news for Hven's residents.

The Great Comet

AFTER ACCEPTING KING FREDERICK'S offer of Hven, Tycho Brahe got to work. Planning the castle took several months. Tycho dedicated the castle to Urania, the Greek Muse of astronomy and celestial forces. It would become famous as Uraniborg, Castle of the Heavens.

Tycho believed that beautiful surroundings inspired great thoughts. He designed his castle to delight the senses. The building was light and graceful. Its brick walls glowed in Hven's rosy sunsets. Fragrant flowers and herbs grew in its gardens. Sweet cherries, pears, apples, and plums hung from trees in orchards enclosed by the castle wall. Birds sang from perches in large cages on Uraniborg's south tower.

Uraniborg was designed with all the latest conveniences. It had the best indoor plumbing in Europe. Pipes from an indoor well carried water to most of its rooms. The pipes also supplied a graceful bronze fountain, which turned slowly and sprayed water into the air in the castle's central hall. The castle walls concealed a secret communications system. Through built-in hollow tubes, Tycho could talk to assistants in different rooms.

Building Uraniborg was an enormous project. Hven laborers dug foundations and hauled dirt and bricks. Skilled builders came to the island to do the finer construction.[1] Sculptors cut limestone for decorations around the windows and doors. Artists painted murals; representations of a variety of plants adorned the ceiling of the summer dining room.

During construction, Tycho often stayed on Hven.

Late in the afternoon of November 13, 1577, Tycho was at his fish ponds. The sun had just set. Tycho looked at the western sky and saw a sight he had waited to see. A fuzzy ball of light shone just above the horizon. Minutes ticked past. The sky darkened as night rolled in. Behind the fuzzy ball, a shimmering tail stretched across the sky. Tycho's first comet had arrived.[2]

Tycho knew about comets, but he had never seen one before. This comet was the first of seven that he and his assistants would observe. The comet's head was stunningly bright. Its tail was twenty-two degrees long. (When you are outside some night, stretch your arm out straight and open your fingers wide. The span from the tip of your thumb to the tip of your little finger is about twenty degrees.[3] Imagine the sight Tycho Brahe saw!)

Tycho folded up a piece of paper and started taking notes. He observed the comet's color: bluish white. He noted that its tail had a reddish tint. He described its exact position, in the constellation Capricorn. Tycho started taking measurements to determine its parallax. Measuring the comet's parallax, Tycho knew, would be more difficult than studying the supernova's parallax. The supernova stayed still. Comets move.

In Tycho's time most people thought that comets came up from the earth. The ancient Greek philosopher Aristotle said they were made of dryness and fatness pulled up from the earth.[4] People believed that comets were like clouds or rainbows.

Comets seen from Earth are small icy bodies that belong to our solar system. Every year they pass through the inner solar system and zip around the sun.

If a comet is large enough and its orbit brings it close enough to Earth, we may see it. Most comets, though, are observed through telescopes. About once every ten years a comet is bright enough to be seen with the naked eye. Brahe's first comet, the great comet of 1577, was visible for three months. In 1997 the bright comet Hale-Bopp was visible for several months.

Many scientists think comets come from two regions beyond the planet Neptune: the Kuiper Belt and the Oort Cloud. Chunks of material left over from the birth of our solar system are believed to drift around in these two distant realms. Occasionally a chunk gets knocked out of position. The sun's gravity pulls it into a new orbit. Because the comet, or chunk, starts so far from the sun, its orbit is a very, very long ellipse. (An ellipse is an oval.) At one end of its elliptical orbit, the comet whips around the sun. Occasionally, small comets vaporize when they travel too close to the sun.

The orbits of some comets go all the way back to the Oort Cloud. Other comets stay closer to the sun.

Over 150 known comets circle the sun every 200 years or less. They are called short-period and intermediate-period comets. Encke's comet orbits the sun every 40 months. Halley's comet circles the sun every 76 years. It travels out as far as Neptune's orbit and then heads back to the sun.

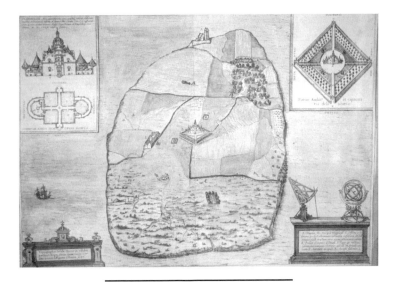

Map of Hven, drawn in 1588. Uraniborg is in the center of the island with cultivated fields and pasture around it. The village of Tuna is above the castle and to the right. Plans of Uraniborg and its grounds are in the upper two corners. Two of Tycho Brahe's observing instruments are depicted in the lower right corner.

Comets have three parts: the nucleus, the coma, and the tail.

The nucleus of a comet is solid. It is usually less than ten miles in diameter. A comet's nucleus is often described as a dirty snowball. It is made of frozen water, dust, and compounds including ammonia and methane.

A comet's coma, or head, is the fuzzy ball of light we see. It consists of dust and gas that has sublimed from the nucleus. *Sublimed* means that it changed directly from a solid to a gas without ever being a liquid. A comet does not make its own light. Like the moon and planets, comets reflect the sun's light.

Most comets have a tail. Like the coma, the tail is made of gas and dust. It always flows away from the sun. The tail of a comet may be more than 100 million miles long. That is greater than the distance from the sun to Earth.

Scientists today are still learning about comets. They observe them and study their orbits and their chemistry. Previously unknown comets are discovered every year. In the year 2012, the *Rosetta* spacecraft is scheduled to visit Comet Wirtanen. A lander from the spacecraft will touch down on the comet's nucleus and examine it.

In Tycho 's time many people feared comets. They believed comets foretold disaster. Tycho believed that by observing comets he could understand them better. He took many measurements of the comet's position. He needed to determine its movement. Once he could plot its movement, he looked for its parallax.

Tycho could not find as much parallax for the comet as he found for the moon. If the comet had less parallax than the moon, Tycho realized, it must be farther away than the moon. If it was farther away than the moon, then it must be part of the heavens. It could not be a "dry fatness" that floated up from Earth.

Studying the comet, Tycho carefully tracked its path. He realized that it crossed several planets' orbits. He did not want to say so, but this meant that the planets could not sit in solid crystal spheres. Solid spheres would shatter when the comet passed through.

The comet of 1577 was visible from November 13 to January 26. Tycho observed it whenever weather permitted. He wrote a report about it for the king.

Tycho's observations of the comet changed his understanding of the heavens. He realized that heavenly spheres could not be solid. He also learned that comets were celestial objects.

Life at Uraniborg

FOR FIVE YEARS URANIBORG GREW. ITS
spires, sculptures, and balconies were finally in
place. At its highest point, seventy-five feet
above the ground, the gold-covered Pegasus
pointed in the direction of the wind. The murals
were painted, trees planted, and fish ponds
stocked. The first assistants were already there.
In 1581 Kirsten and the children moved in.

Uraniborg was everything that Tycho
imagined. With its art, gardens, and gracious
rooms, it was a beautiful home. It was also the
most advanced astronomical observatory in the
world.

The castle's north and south towers were observatories. Their roofs opened. Large instruments were installed in them. In the south tower stood the large azimuth semicircle. With this instrument, Tycho and his assistants could follow the movements of celestial objects as they crossed the southern sky. In the north tower, instruments were positioned to study the stars in the northern sky. Small observatories next to the towers held instruments that could be used inside or outdoors on broad balconies.

Tycho's instruments were the most accurate observing tools of his time. He designed instruments over several years at Uraniborg, adding new and more accurate ones to his observatories.

One of Tycho's most famous instruments was his mural quadrant. This quadrant was used to measure altitude. The term *quadrant* comes from the instrument's form: it is a 90-degree arc, a quarter of a circle. The radius of Tycho's mural quadrant was six feet nine inches. The arc was made of brass. Degrees and minutes of arc were

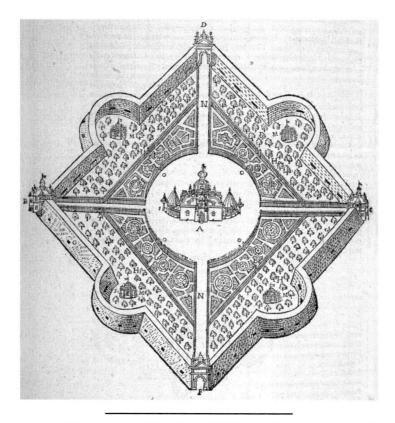

Layout of the grounds of Uraniborg (1596). A wall enclosed the castle complex. It was precisely laid out with its corners at the north, south, east, and west. North is to the right in this plan. The north and south tower observatories are under the cone-shaped roofs on either side of the castle.

precisely inscribed on it. It was attached to a wall that faced due south. High up on the intersecting wall, a small hole revealed a sliver of sky.

Three people usually worked together with the mural quadrant. Two of them, the clock-watcher and the scribe, held candles as they worked. Other than the candlelight, the room would be dark. The third person, the observer, observed the stars through the hole in the wall. He moved the quadrant's sliding eyepiece up and down the arc to line it up with the object he was studying. When he had the planet or star lined up in the sight, he signaled the others. The clock-watcher noted the exact time on two clocks. The scribe wrote down the time of the observation and the position of the sliding sight on the arc. That position told them the altitude of the star.[1]

Besides being useful, the mural quadrant was elegant. Tycho considered it the artistic masterpiece of Uraniborg.[2] An exquisite mural, the combined work of three famous artists, filled the space inside the quadrant. Tycho is handsomely portrayed in the mural, pointing to the wall. The painted Tycho points to the real sighting hole. A dog rests by his feet. Some of his instruments and globes are depicted. Tiny paintings of King Frederick and Queen Sophie hang in the mural. Uraniborg's observatories, library, and laboratories fill the background. In all the painted rooms, painted assistants are hard at work.

Assistants were very important to Tycho's research. Tycho needed thousands of observations. He wanted to map hundreds of stars. Decoding the wandering of the planets required countless observations. The sun, moon, and comets needed study as well. It was far more work than Tycho could possibly do himself.

Usually about ten assistants were at Uraniborg at a time. Many came from the University of Copenhagen. Some were from Germany and Holland. A few came from as far as France, Scotland, and England.

The assistants were not paid to work for Tycho. Their reward was learning from him. At Uraniborg they used Tycho's instruments. They learned his procedures for observations. They observed with him and heard his thoughts about the heavenly scheme.

The assistants also helped Tycho experiment with alchemy, a kind of early chemistry.

Mural quadrant engraving from the Mechanica. *In the mural, behind Tycho, you can see observatories at the top, studies in the middle, and alchemy laboratories at the bottom.*

Laboratories filled Uraniborg's basement. Part of alchemy dealt with trying to change substances into other substances. Some alchemists were obsessed with turning worthless metals into gold. Alchemy also dealt with healing and medicine, and this seems to have been Tycho's greater interest.[3]

Over the years, about one hundred assistants came to Uraniborg. Some stayed only a few weeks. Others stayed for years. Peter Flemlose was at Uraniborg from 1577 to 1588.[4] Flemlose worked extensively on Tycho's observations of the fixed stars. He often trained new assistants. Many of Tycho's observations are in Flemlose's handwriting. Christian Longomontanus was at Hven from 1589 to 1597.[5] He was the son of peasants but was educated at the University of Copenhagen. Longomontanus became a very respected astronomer. For many years after Uraniborg, he taught at the University of Copenhagen.

Tycho called his household his familia. *Familia* means "family" in Latin. He did not truly mean that they were a family. He meant that they were all under his care.[6] Living in Tycho's Uraniborg, the familia shared many routines.

Days on Hven started early. The household rose at three or four o'clock in the morning. Porridge or herring was a typical Uraniborg breakfast.[7] After breakfast everyone worked. In the winter they could observe for hours before the sun came up. In December, the sun rises at Hven after eight in the morning.

Meals were served in the spacious Winter Room. A great oak table sat at its center. Bookshelves and benches were arranged along the walls. This was the warmest room in the castle; it was heated by a large tile stove. In the style of the time, the Winter Room was also Tycho's bedroom. At night he tucked himself into the four-poster bed that stood in one corner.[8]

The household ate lunch at around ten in the morning. It would be a large meal of fish, meat, bread, and vegetables. After lunch they were back to work.[9] During the day, assistants worked

This 1882 painting by Heinrich Hansen is based on engravings of Stjerneborg. The chambers of Stjerneborg were built underground with the instruments positioned under roofs that turned.

on calculations and alchemy. Tycho might be designing instruments, writing books, or writing letters. He corresponded with astronomers, mathematicians, and old friends across Europe. He stayed in contact with students and professors he had known in Germany. He exchanged letters with nobles and scholars who shared his interest in the heavens.

Late in the afternoon dinner was served. Tycho, Kirsten, their children, the assistants, and guests would again gather in the Winter Room.

Dinner was a grand meal. Huge quantities of food were served in noble households like Tycho's. The menu might include salmon, lobster, lamb, beef, turnips, beets, bread, cheese, cakes and fresh fruits. Tablecloths covered the oak table. Places were set with plates and huge napkins. At feasts a knife and spoon would be set at each place, but at daily dinners guests would bring their own utensils. Servants presented the food in large silver serving dishes. Forks were used for serving, not eating. The diners ate with knife, spoon, and their hands.[10]

Dinner was social and work time. The household discussed the day's accomplishments and planned what was ahead. A musician would play the lute during the meal. On cloudy evenings the group might stay at the dinner table for hours.[11]

Nighttime observing sessions were often scheduled after dinner. Unusual events brought everybody back to work. Tycho's notes show that during lunar eclipses, three teams observed in different observatories all at the same time.[12]

Soon after Uraniborg was complete, Tycho realized that he needed even more observing space. In 1584 he added new observatories. He named the addition Stjerneborg, Castle of the Stars. It had five observation chambers, all built underground like cellars. Circular roofs over the chambers turned on little wheels. Slices of the roofs opened. In these observatories, the instruments sat on solid ground. With the turning roofs, they had 360-degree views of the sky. This design sheltered the observers and instruments from Hven's strong winds.

Astronomy at Hven

"BY THE GRACE OF GOD IT CAME ABOUT," wrote Tycho, "that there was hardly any day or night with clear weather that we did not get a great many, and very accurate astronomical observations of the fixed stars as well as of all the planets, and also of the comets that appeared during that time, seven of which were carefully observed in the sky from that place. In this way observations were industriously made during 21 years."[1]

To get a better idea of Tycho Brahe's astronomy, we will very briefly look at seven of his projects on Hven.

Celestial Globe and Star Catalog

A list of star positions is called a star catalog. Before Brahe's observations, the catalog in use was from Ptolemy's time. It was 1,400 years old. It been copied over and over again by hand. By the 1500s, it had many errors.[2]

One of Tycho's biggest projects was to establish a new star catalog. He would list the stars in the catalog. He would also show their positions on a globe.

Tycho saw this project as one of the most important steps toward establishing a new astronomy. He wanted his information about the fixed stars to be as accurate as possible, especially because the positions of the planets were measured from the stars. To assure this, Tycho and his assistants recorded many, many observations.

The positions of the stars can be described almost the same way we describe the location of places on Earth. On Earth we use latitude and longitude. In the heavens, positions are described in declination and right ascension.

Tycho Brahe's celestial globe. It was almost six feet in diameter and had one thousand stars represented in their positions. Constellations were depicted on it as well.

Complex mathematical calculations are required to translate observed measurements to these coordinates. Tycho and his assistants spent much time doing calculations.

Tycho's celestial globe was a model of the heavenly sphere. Stars were precisely engraved on its gleaming brass surface. The globe was six feet in diameter. Almost every star that could be seen from Hven was on it. The globe was the centerpiece of Uraniborg's library. A silk cover protected it from dust.

For several years Tycho and his assistants carefully observed 777 stars. They checked and rechecked their observations and calculations. Later, Tycho decided that 1,000 stars would be more impressive. His assistants measured many more stars. Some of these were very faint and hard to see. These stars were added to the catalog and globe.

Planetary Observations

From the time Tycho observed the conjunction of Jupiter and Saturn in 1563, he wanted accurate observations of the planets. At Hven, he collected much of the information he needed. He methodically studied the five planets he could see: Mercury, Venus, Mars, Jupiter, and Saturn. He recorded their positions as they appeared to wander across the sky. Tycho noted planetary conjunctions and oppositions. Opposition is when a planet is 180 degrees away from another heavenly body, usually the sun.

Tycho was fascinated by Mars. He suspected that Mars was sometimes closer than the sun to Earth, as Copernicus had predicted.[3] He tried hard to measure parallax for Mars to prove this. Unfortunately for Tycho, Mars is so far from Earth that its diurnal parallax cannot be observed without a telescope. Although he could not detect its parallax, Tycho kept measuring Mars. Tycho was right, although he never found the proof he wanted.

In his efforts to understand Mars, he made many observations of it. These observations shaped the history of astronomy. They provided one of Tycho's assistants, Johannes Kepler, with the information he needed to figure out the shape of the planets' orbits.

The Motion of the Moon

If you carefully watch the moon, you will see that it does not follow the same course across the sky each time it goes around Earth. That is because its orbit is tilted relative to Earth. Earth's axis is also tilted relative to its own orbit around the sun. You can draw the apparent orbit of the sun and the moon as circles on a celestial globe. The two circles cross at two points. These intersections are called nodes.

Tycho made several discoveries about the moon. Between 1582 and 1595, he made approximately 300 observations of the moon. From these observations Tycho first discovered that the moon's orbit was tilted more than Ptolemy had calculated. Then he realized that it was sometimes tilted less than Ptolemy had calculated. Tycho discovered that the tilt, or inclination, of the moon's orbit varies. He recognized that if the inclination of the orbit varied, then the nodes would vary, too.[4]

Eclipses of the sun and moon only happen near these lunar nodes. For a solar eclipse, the moon must pass directly between Earth and the sun. For a lunar eclipse, Earth must pass in front of the sun so that its shadow falls on the moon. Tycho's observations and theory helped explain when eclipses would occur.

Tycho's lunar theory is still respected as an important discovery in the history of astronomy.

The Movement of the Sun

Tycho did not leave the sun out of his studies. On Hven, he regularly observed solstices and equinoxes.

Summer solstice occurs when the sun reaches its northernmost point. This occurs each year around June 21. In the Northern Hemisphere, this is the longest day of the year. Winter solstice is the sun's southernmost annual position. Winter solstice is usually on December 22.

The equinoxes occur on approximately March 21 and September 23. On these two dates, day and night are the same length.

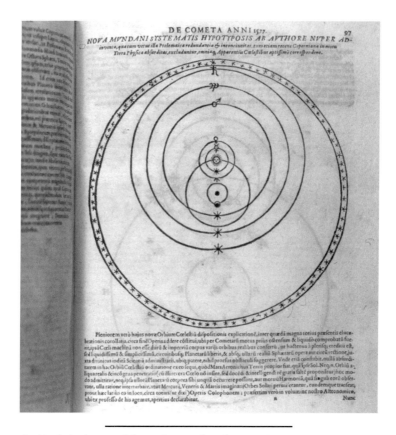

In Brahe's theory of the universe, the planets Mercury, Venus, Mars, Jupiter, and Saturn revolved around the sun. The sun, in turn, revolved around Earth. In this representation of his system, Earth is shown as the black dot in the center.

For several years Tycho devoted one full day in June to the sun.[5] He tracked its path across the sky. He was trying to measure light refraction. Light refraction is the bending of a ray of light when it passes from one medium to another. You see the effects of light refraction at sunset. The sun looks bigger than it looked overhead. When the sun's rays pass through a broad slice of Earth's atmosphere, they bend and the sun appears larger.

Many of Tycho's refraction calculations were quite accurate. Some were not.

Astronomical Instruments

Tycho devised the best astronomical instruments that existed before the invention of the telescope. He started designing instruments in 1569 while he was in Germany.

At Hven, he made quadrants, armillaries, sextants, azimuth circles, and more. His instruments measured angles, altitudes, and positions of objects as they crossed the sky. Tycho invented special sighting devices so that his instruments could be precisely aimed at a star or planet. He figured out a new way to measure small fractions of a degree on a curve. With some instruments, Tycho consistently took measurements that were accurate to one-sixtieth of a degree.[6]

(To get an idea of this accuracy, look at the sky on a starry night. Stretch one arm in front of you. Make a fist and point your thumb up. The width of your thumb covers approximately 2 degrees of sky.[7] Imagine being able to accurately measure angles 1/120 the width of your thumb.)

In 1597, Tycho published his *Astronomiae instauratae mechanica* ("Instruments for a new astronomy"). Many of his instruments are illustrated and described in the *Mechanica*.

The Tychonic Universe

Tycho Brahe's observations showed him that Ptolemy's model of the universe was wrong. He realized that the heavenly spheres could not be solid. His observations showed that the planets did not move as Ptolemy thought. Still, he did not believe Copernicus's theory that Earth orbited the sun.

Tycho proposed his own system of the universe. Earth was at the center of the Tychonic

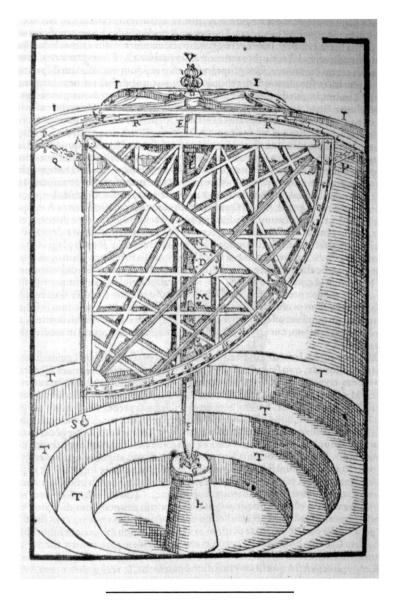

The revolving azimuth quadrant engraving from Mechanica. *This instrument was installed in one of the underground Stjerneborg observing chambers. You can see the iron pillar on which the instrument was mounted.*

model. The moon orbited Earth. Farther out, the sun circled Earth. In Tycho's system, the planets circled the sun. The stars were in the farthest sphere, rotating around Earth.

Today we know that Tycho's model was not correct. However, in his time, it was a step toward a new view of the universe. Tycho's observations helped Johannes Kepler make the next step.

Publishing

In Tycho's time books were changing the world. The printing press was invented by Johannes Gutenberg around 1450, less than one hundred years before Tycho Brahe was born. Before Gutenberg's invention, books were copied by hand. It was a slow process.

Gutenberg's invention advanced science. His printing press made it possible to make many copies that were exactly the same. Printed accounts of discoveries could be read by many people. Scientists in different countries could study exactly the same information. New ideas spread faster than ever before.

At Uraniborg, Tycho had a printing press, print shop, and paper mill. He published his own books. He also published the works of his friends. He published a book of Danish history written by his former tutor and lifelong friend Anders Vedel.

Tycho planned to write a major work about his new astronomy. In 1588 he published *De mundi aetherei recentioribus phaenomenis* ("Concerning the more recent phenomena of the ethereal world"). The book was a detailed account of the comet of 1577. It explained his observations and measurements of parallax. His Tychonic model of the universe was presented in one chapter.

On Hven, Tycho wrote and published several sections of his *Astronomiae Instauratae progymnasmata* ("Introduction to a new astronomy"). This 900-page book would include his solar observations, his star catalog, his lunar theory, and his observations of the supernova. The finished book was published in 1602, the year after Tycho Brahe died.

Leaving Denmark

DURING TYCHO BRAHE'S EARLY YEARS AT Hven, King Frederick supported him generously. Besides giving Tycho the island, the king "abundantly defrayed the expenses" of Uraniborg, just as he had promised.

Every year Frederick paid Tycho from the royal treasury. He also gave him other fiefs. Tycho was paid taxes by the people who lived on these lands. Some responsibilities came with these grants. At Kullengaard, Tycho was supposed to hire someone to keep the lighthouse fire burning.[1] The lighthouse warned ships about dangerous rocks. At Roskilde, Tycho was supposed to keep the chapel in good repair. Kings of Denmark were buried in the chapel.[2] With his annual payment from the king and taxes from his fiefs, Tycho's income was enormous.

Tycho showed his appreciation to King Frederick. He reported celestial events such as comets and eclipses to the king. He wrote interpretations of these events for him.

When Frederick's first son, Christian IV, was born in 1577, Tycho wrote a detailed birth horoscope for the prince. When the king had two more sons, Tycho wrote horoscopes for them, too. His horoscope for Prince Ulrich still exists. It is 300 pages long, all handwritten by Tycho. It is wrapped in a green velvet cover. The positions of the planets and stars on the day of the baby's birth are described. Tycho wrote in great detail how this celestial picture might influence the prince.[3]

Whether Frederick ever visited Uraniborg is unknown. His wife, Queen Sophie, visited twice. Her first visit was in 1586. Tycho's mother, Beate Bille, came with her. Tycho showed Sophie all around his castle. They toured the observatories in the towers and at Stjerneborg. Tycho showed her his celestial globe and mural quadrant. They wandered through his orchards and gardens. Tycho put on a great feast for the queen. Anders Vedel was at Uraniborg. He entertained Sophie with stories about Denmark's history. The royal visit was an enormous success. Sophie was charmed by Tycho and his Castle of the Heavens.[4] She came back to the island for another delightful visit later that year.

In 1588 King Frederick II died. Tycho went to his funeral. Frederick was buried in the chapel in Roskilde.

Things might have changed sooner for Tycho, but Prince Christian was only ten years old at the time of his father's death. Until Christian turned eighteen and became king, Denmark was ruled by a council of noblemen. Tycho's brothers Steen and Jørgen and many cousins held high positions in government. Manderup Parsberg, whose sword had cut off Brahe's nose, was on the ruling council. Parsberg and Brahe had become good friends as adults, and Parsberg was rather

This engraving of Tycho Brahe offers a clearer picture of how his prosthetic nose appeared.

sensitive about their youthful duel.[5] The council continued to support Tycho and Uraniborg.

Hven was a busy place through the 1580s and early 1590s. Tycho's astronomy was thriving. Tycho was observing and writing. His assistants handled routine work for him. Tycho worked on his solar theory, lunar theory, and star catalog. He published *De mundi,* his book about the comet. He published part of his daily meteorological journal. Every single day for fifteen years, Tycho's assistants recorded weather and events in this journal.

Prince Christian visited Uraniborg when he was fifteen years old. It was a pleasant visit. Tycho gave the prince a small wind-up globe.

Christian was not, however, as interested in astronomy as his father had been. As Christian grew up, Tycho's situation began to change. His astronomy and his lifestyle were costing the government a lot of money. He had failed to fulfill many duties that came with Frederick's generous gifts. The chapel in Roskilde needed work. Tycho was told to fix it, but he did not order repairs. The Hven islanders complained to the government that Tycho treated them unfairly. Tycho had a nasty lawsuit with a tenant in one of his manor houses.

Around the same time Tycho began to worry about his children. His four girls and two boys

A portrait of King Christian IV of Denmark, painted by Pieter Isaacsz in 1612.

were growing up. Their futures were limited by their common birth. As commoners, they could not marry nobles and they could not inherit Tycho's estate. Tycho had tried to make a special arrangement for the children to inherit Hven. Frederick supposedly supported the idea, but he died before an agreement was signed.

In 1594 Tycho's eldest daughter, Magdalene, was engaged to marry one of his former assistants, Gellius Sascerides. Sascerides was a commoner, but he was well educated and Brahe thought he had a promising future. As the wedding was planned, Tycho and Sascerides quarreled. The quarrel may have been about money or about the bridegroom's responsibilities to Tycho. Sascerides canceled the wedding. He then spread cruel rumors about Tycho and Magdalene.[6]

At around the same time as Magdalene's problems, Prince Christian went to Roskilde to visit his father's tomb. Tycho had not repaired the chapel roof. It was ready to collapse. Rain dripped in near the graves of the dead kings of Denmark. The prince was furious.[7]

In August 1596, Christian IV was crowned King of Denmark. Tycho attended the celebration. It was immediately clear that Christian would not support Tycho. Tycho's payment from the royal treasury stopped. A government committee went to Hven to investigate the islanders' complaints.[8]

On March 15, 1597, Tycho took his last observation at Uraniborg. He ordered his servants to pack his belongings. Two weeks later, he left his island.

First Tycho moved to his house in Copenhagen. Life was no happier there. Rumors from Magdalene's engagement were still whispered. King Christian would not allow Tycho to take observations from the city wall.

On June 2, 1597, Tycho left Denmark. Horse-drawn wagons and carriages loaded with furniture, clothing, books, manuscripts, thousands of observations, a few small astronomical instruments, and his printing press accompanied him. So did Kirsten, the children, a few assistants, and more than a dozen servants.

10

Exile

TYCHO BRAHE'S FIRST STOP WAS ROSTOCK, the city where he had lost his nose. From Rostock he wrote a long letter to King Christian. Tycho reminded the young king that his father, Frederick, had promised to support him. He challenged Christian to keep his father's word. If Christian did not support him, Tycho said, he would look for another prince who was interested.[1] Before Tycho received an answer from Christian, plague spread through Rostock. Tycho and his household left the city to avoid the deadly disease.

Next, Tycho and his family visited an old friend, Viceroy Heinrich Rantzau. Rantzau was a wealthy German nobleman who was interested in astronomy. His family owned seventy castles and manor houses.[2] Rantzau loaned Tycho his castle at Wandsbeck. King Christian's response reached Brahe at Wandsbeck. Christian did not ask Tycho to return to Denmark. Instead, he scolded him for his arrogant letter.

A little sad, Tycho realized he needed to plan his life outside of Denmark. He could stay at Wandsbeck for a while. He had money from his inheritances. Several of the chests he had brought with him were filled with gold, silver, and jewels. Still, studying astronomy as he had at Uraniborg would cost more than his personal wealth. He needed a new royal sponsor. Tycho wondered which of Europe's kings would support him best.

Rudolph II was his choice. Rudolph was emperor of the Holy Roman Empire. The empire covered one-quarter of all Europe. It was made up of many kingdoms. Its boundaries included parts of countries that are now Germany, France, Austria, the Czech Republic, Switzerland, and more. Emperor Rudolph lived in Prague.

Tycho was as thorough in his plan to win Rudolph's favor as he was in his astronomy. He prepared grand gifts for Rudolph. The gifts showed off Tycho's achievements.

Tycho published his *Astronomiae instauratae mechanica* ("Instruments for the restored astronomy"). With twenty-two magnificently engraved woodcuts, the *Mechanica* illustrated Tycho's instruments. The great wall mural, his celestial globe, and many others were beautifully portrayed. (The pictures are so exact that working models can be made from them.) Tycho Brahe dedicated the *Mechanica* to Rudolph.

Tycho had his assistants carefully copy by hand his catalog of 1,000 stars.[3] He dedicated the star catalog to Rudolph. He also dedicated to Rudolph a chart of the movements of the sun and moon.

As Tycho prepared to gain the emperor's support, he was ready to start his next research project. He wanted to work on his planetary theory. From Uraniborg, Tycho had many years of observations of the planets. He still had to do many calculations to interpret them. Tycho knew he needed assistants who were very good at mathematics. At Wandsbeck, he received a letter from a man who could help him.

Johannes Kepler lived in Graz, which is now in Austria. He was a gifted mathematician. Kepler believed that there was a mathematical order to the universe. In 1596 he wrote a book called the *Mysterium cosmographicum* ("Cosmic mystery"). He sent a copy to Tycho and asked for his comments.

In *Mysterium cosmographicum*, Kepler proposed mathematical ratios for the dimensions of the planets' orbits. His theory accepted and built upon Copernicus's model of a sun-centered universe. He argued in his book that the sun was at the center of the planetary system and that it must provide the force that kept the planets in motion.[4]

Tycho read the book. Kepler's theories were very different from Tycho's beliefs about the positions of the sun and Earth in the universe. Still, he was impressed by Kepler's mathematical genius. He wrote a detailed letter back to Kepler

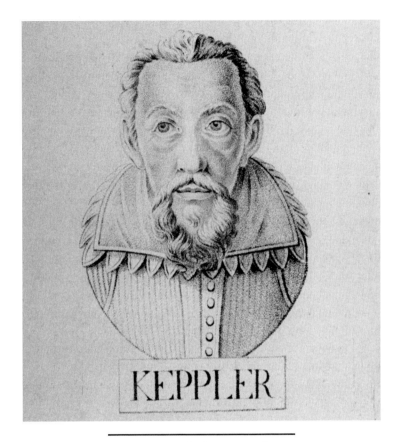

A portrait of Johannes Kepler.

and suggested they meet. Almost two years passed before they finally got together.

In 1599 Emperor Rudolph asked Tycho to come to Prague. Their meeting was everything Tycho might have wished. Tycho wrote afterward that Rudolph said "How agreeable my arrival was for him and that he promised to support me and my research, all the while smiling in the most kindly way so that his whole face beamed with benevolence."[5]

Emperor Rudolph offered Tycho his choice of several castles. He promised to pay for observatories at the castle. Tycho could have a new Uraniborg. Rudolph offered him a large salary.

Rudolph's enthusiasm improved life for Tycho's family. Kirsten Jørgensdatter and the children were treated as nobles in the Holy Roman Empire. Tycho eventually chose to take the castle of Benatky, about six hours by carriage from Prague.

In early 1600 Johannes Kepler arrived. Tycho believed that Kepler could be a great help to him with his planetary theory. Kepler knew that Tycho had thousands of observations of the heavens. He knew that these were the most accurate observations that existed.

"What influenced me the most," Kepler wrote, "was the hope of completing my study of the harmony of the world—something that I

Tycho Brahe's observatories: A. center, Uraniborg; B. upper left, Wandsbeck; C. upper right, Benatky; D. lower left, Imperial Gardens in Prague; E. lower right, Jacob Kurtz's house, the last house where Tycho lived in Prague.

have long contemplated and that I would be able to contemplate only if Tycho were to rebuild astronomy or if I could use his observations."[6]

Kepler and Tycho tried to work out an arrangement. Kepler wanted to be treated as an independent scholar. Tycho wanted Kepler to be his assistant. They disagreed about Kepler's salary, responsibilities, and housing. Kepler believed in Copernicus's theory that Earth revolved around the sun. Tycho believed in his own Earth-centered Tychonic theory. The relationship between Tycho and Kepler was stormy, but both men saw advantages to working together.

Kepler stayed at Benatky for a few months. Then he went back to Graz, but political and religious problems were brewing there.

In December 1600, Rudolph decided he wanted Tycho to be closer to him. He moved Tycho and family to a castle in Prague. Kepler and his wife and daughter joined Tycho there early the next year.

Tycho put Kepler in charge of calculating the movement of Mars. In August 1601, Tycho and

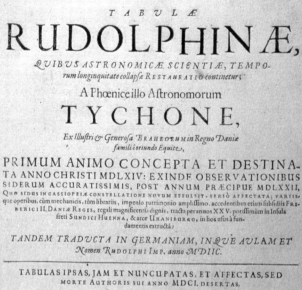

TABULÆ
RUDOLPHINÆ,
QUIBUS ASTRONOMICÆ SCIENTIÆ, TEMPO-
rum longinquitate collapsæ RESTAURATIO continetur;

A Phœnice illo Astronomorum
TYCHONE,
Ex Illustri & Generosa BRAHEORUM in Regno Daniæ
familiâ oriundo Equite,

PRIMUM ANIMO CONCEPTA ET DESTINA-
TA ANNO CHRISTI MDLXIV: EXINDE OBSERVATIONIBUS
SIDERUM ACCURATISSIMIS, POST ANNUM PRÆCIPUE MDLXXII,
Quo SIDUS IN CASSIOPEIÆ CONSTELLATIONE NOVUM EFFULSIT - SERIÒ AFFECTATA; VARIIS-
que operibus, cùm mechanicis, tùm librariis, impenso patrimonio amplissimo. accedentibus etiam subsidiis FRI-
BERICI II, DANIÆ REGIS, regali magnificentiâ dignis, tractâ per annos XXV. potissimùm in Insula
freti SUNDICI HUENNA, & arce URANIBURGO, in hos usus à fun-
damentis extructâ:

TANDEM TRADUCTA IN GERMANIAM, INQUE AULAM ET
Nomen RUDOLPHI IMP. anno MDIIC.

TABULAS IPSAS, JAM ET NUNCUPATAS, ET AFFECTAS, SED
MORTE AUTHORIS SUI ANNO MDCI. DESERTAS,

JUSSU ET STIPENDIIS FRETUS TRIUM IMPPP.

RUDOLPHI, MATTHIÆ, FERDINANDI,
ANNITENTIBUS HÆREDIBUS BRAHEANIS; EX FUNDAMENTIS OB-
servationum relictarum; ad exemplum ferè partium jam exstructarum; continuis multorum annorum spe-
culationibus, & computationibus, primùm PRAGÆ Bohemorum continuavit; deinde LINCII,
Superioris Austriæ Metropoli, subsidiis etiam Ill. Provincialium adjutus, perfecit, ab-
solvit; adq; causarum & calculi perenni formulam traduxit.

IOANNES KEPLERUS,
TYCHONI primùm à RUDOLPHO II Imp. adjunctus calculi minister; indéq;
Trium ordine Imppp. Mathematicus:

Qui idem de speciali mandato FERDINANDI II. IMP.
petentibus instantibúsq; Hæredibus,

Opus hoc ad usus præsentium & posteritatis, typis, numericis propriis, cæteris, & prælo
JONÆ SAURII, Reip. Ulmanæ Typographi, in publicum extulit, &
Typographicis operis ULMÆ curator assuit.

Cum Privilegiis, IMP. & Regum Rerúmq; publ. vivo TYCHONI ejúsq; Hæredibus,
& speciali Imperatorio, ipsi KEPLERO concesso, ad Annos XXX.
ANNO M. DC. XXVII.

The Rudolphine Tables *were begun by Tycho Brahe using his vast collection of observations. They were completed by Johannes Kepler and published in 1627, twenty-six years after Brahe's death.*

Kepler met with Emperor Rudolph. Tycho told Rudolph that Kepler would be his assistant in a great project. They would develop complete tables of planetary motion. Tycho would name them the *Rudolphine Tables* in honor of the emperor.

On the evening of October 13, 1601, Tycho attended a grand banquet. He ate and drank. It was considered rude to excuse oneself from the dinner table before the host left. Tycho was painfully uncomfortable, but he stayed. When the party finally ended, he could not urinate. He was in agony. Back at his castle, he took mercury to try to cure himself. Tycho Brahe died on October 24, 1601 of mercury poisoning and urine in his blood.[7]

A huge funeral was held for Tycho in Prague. Noblemen, ladies, and judges accompanied his family in an impressive funeral procession. People lined the streets and crowded into the cathedral to honor his memory.

Tycho was buried in Teyn Cathedral in Prague. A life-sized statue of Tycho in his armor and his motto, "To be, not to seem," are on his tomb.

11

Tycho Brahe's Legacy

AFTER TYCHO BRAHE'S DEATH, HIS family stayed in Prague. Rudolph's admiration of Tycho gave them great respect in the Holy Roman Empire. They were treated as nobles.

Kirsten and the children inherited Tycho's wealth, his manuscripts, his observations, and his instruments. Rudolph bought Tycho Brahe's instruments from them. He offered to pay a spectacular price. Although he never finally paid the full amount, the family received many generous payments from him. Kirsten bought a large country house. She lived there until she died in 1604. She was buried next to Tycho in Teyn Cathedral.

All Tycho Brahe's children except Magdalene married nobles. Magdalene remained single. One daughter, Elizabeth, married Frans Tengnagel, a nobleman from the Netherlands who was one of Tycho's assistants. None of Tycho's children went back to Denmark to live.

Uraniborg did not fare as well as Tycho's family. Without Tycho, the castle was neglected. King Christian did not maintain it or use it for astronomy. He granted the fief to other Danish nobles. Bricks were torn from Uraniborg's walls to build a new manor house on the island.[1] Tycho's castle crumbled.

In 1658 Denmark lost many lands to Sweden. Knutstrup, Roskilde, and Hven all became part of Sweden, and are Swedish today.

In the twentieth century, archaeologists excavated parts of Uraniborg. Circular foundations of the Stjerneborg observation chambers were still intact under dirt and debris.

Tycho's plans for his gardens and orchards were carefully researched in the 1990s. One of Uraniborg's gardens was replanted in the same

Archaeological excavation of one of Tycho's observing chambers at Stjerneborg. It is still recognizable under dirt and debris. The revolving azimuth quadrant stood in this chamber or one similar to it.

design and with the same plants that Tycho enjoyed.[2]

Tycho's greatest legacy was his astronomy. His achievements were impressive. His star catalog was the best in the world in his time. His observations of the supernova and comet revised earlier beliefs about the universe. His lunar theory correctly explained aspects of the moon's movement. Tycho's innovations and instrument designs helped observational astronomy be more precise. Finally, Tycho's planetary observations helped Johannes Kepler figure out the orbits of the planets.

A few days after Tycho died, Rudolph II appointed Kepler to be imperial mathematician. Kepler had the use of Tycho's observations. He continued to work on planetary theory. In 1609 Kepler published his first two laws of planetary motion. He discovered that the planets travel in elliptical orbits around the sun.

Kepler always honored Tycho's memory. In 1627, he published the *Rudolphine Tables*. Tycho Tycho listed as the author of the work. The cover reads that Tycho was assisted by Johannes Kepler.

Tycho hoped that through his work, astronomy "might finally be restored to wholeness and handed down to posterity more correct than at any time before."[3] Tycho achieved that goal. His superb observations and insightful theories improved astronomy and helped humankind better understand Earth's place in the universe.

Activities

Parallax

Parallax is the apparent movement of a near object relative to a distant one. It is the result of observing from two different positions. When Tycho Brahe observed *diurnal parallax*, he was observing from two different points during Earth's daily rotation. You can observe parallax from two different points on your head.

Try this experiment to see where parallax appears greater and smaller.

You will need:

    A ruler

    A cereal box

    A tabletop

Procedure:

1. Set the ruler on edge at one end of the table. The numbers should be facing the table.

2. Place your chin on the opposite end of the table so that you are facing the ruler. Close your left eye.

3. Position the cereal box so that its right edge lines up with the left edge of the ruler.

4. Open your left eye and close your right eye.

5. Read the ruler measurement at the right edge of the box.

6. Write down the number of inches of observed parallax.

7. Repeat the experiment with the cereal box farther away. Write down your observation.

8. Move the cereal box closer and record your observation. Where did you see the greatest difference?

Explanation

Parallax can be a valuable measuring tool. You can see that you measure greater parallax when the cereal box is close to you and less parallax when it is farther away. Without a telescope, Tycho Brahe could observe diurnal parallax of

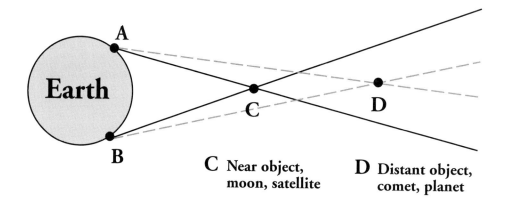

A

Earth

B

C Near object,
moon, satellite

D Distant object,
comet, planet

This diagram illustrates the relative parallax of close and distant objects in space from Earth.

the moon and comets. When he could not detect parallax for the supernova, he knew that it was very far away, farther than the moon.

Fruit Bowl Opposition

Tycho Brahe recorded many observations of planets when they were in opposition to the sun. *Opposition* means that two celestial bodies appear to be 180 degrees away from each other. Tycho suspected that when Mars was in opposition to the sun, it was closer to Earth than the sun was at the same time.

You can make a model to see if he was right.

You will need:

> 3 round pieces of fruit; a grapefruit, an apple, and a lemon work well
>
> 50 inches of string
>
> A ruler
>
> 3 toothpicks
>
> A pair of scissors

Procedure:

1. Cut a piece of string 20 inches long. Cut another piece 30 inches long.

2. Tie one end of each string around a toothpick. Push the toothpick into the top of the grapefruit.

3. Tie the other end of the shorter string around another toothpick. Push the toothpick into the top of the apple.

4. Tie the remaining toothpick to the end of the longer string. Push the toothpick into the lemon. The lemon and apple are now each connected to the grapefruit by separate strings. Each string will serve as the radius for the fruit's orbit.

5. Extending the strings, line up the lemon and apple on one side of the grapefruit. Look at the distances between them.

6. With the longer string extended, move the lemon along its orbit to the other side of the grapefruit. Stop when the apple, grapefruit, and lemon are in a straight line. Look at the distance again. How far is the lemon from the apple?

Explanation:

In your model, the grapefruit is the sun. The apple is Earth. The lemon is Mars. The strings very roughly show the relative distances of these planets from the sun. In this model, two inches of string represent 10 million miles. (Earth's average distance from the sun is 93 million miles. Mars's average distance from the sun is 142 million miles.) Your fruit is not at all to scale with the sun's and planets' sizes. If the sun were to scale with the string, instead of being a grapefruit, it would be a little bigger than a golf ball.

When Mars is in opposition to the sun, it is on the opposite side of Earth from the sun. At this point it is about 49 million miles from Earth. The sun is an average distance of 93 million miles from Earth. Tycho Brahe was right that at times Mars is closer to Earth than Earth is to the sun. (Interestingly, even with his superb instruments, he was unable to measure Mars's parallax to prove this. Forty-nine million miles is a great distance. To measure the diurnal parallax of Mars, you need a telescope.)

Observing the Sky

Some parts of observing were easier for Tycho Brahe than for us. His sky was darker. There were no streetlights or car lights or house lights reflecting in the night sky. In cities today it can be difficult to see the stars because the sky is so bright. This is called light pollution.

To understand some of Tycho Brahe's fascination for studying the sky, go outside and try it yourself.

You will need:

A view of the sky on a clear night

A chair or small table

Measuring altitude

Tycho Brahe worked hard to measure the altitude of stars as precisely as he could. Altitude is the height of a celestial body above the horizon. Once your eyes have adjusted to the dark, pick out one star, fairly high in the sky. You can use your hand to measure the angular distance above the horizon.

Stretch your arm out full length and open your hand wide. Your open hand covers about 20 degrees from the tip of your little finger to the tip of your thumb. Your closed fist covers about 10 degrees, and your thumb about 2 degrees.

Use your hands to try to measure your star's elevation above the horizon. A star straight overhead will be at 90 degrees.

Movement of the Heavens

This activity will work best if you are observing the moon. You will need a lawn chair or small table that you can easily move. Lie on the ground in a comfortable position. You will need to hold your body very still when you start observing. Place the chair or table in a position where the moon is lined up along one side of it. Lie down and watch the moon move. It will travel the distance of its own diameter in about two minutes. If it is rising, it will appear to move up. If it is setting, it will appear to move down. If you are faced south, the moon may appear to move sideways. Try watching the movement of the stars relative to your chair or table, too.

You know that the movement you are seeing is caused by Earth's rotation. Earth spins on its axis each day and the sun, moon, stars, and planets appear to rise and set. Tycho Brahe had heard theories about Earth's rotation, but he did not think they made sense. He was observing the same things that you can see. By observing them, he was trying to figure out how the universe worked.

Chronology

1546—Tyge Brahe, later known as Tycho Brahe, born in Knutstrup, Denmark, December 14.

1547 or 1548— "Kidnapped" by his father's brother, Jørgen Brahe.

1553—Begins grammar school education.

1559—Begins studies at the University of Copenhagen.

1561—Buys his first astronomy book.

1562—Goes to Leipzig, Germany, to study law.

1563—Observes a conjunction of Jupiter and Saturn on August 24.

1566—Nose cut off in a sword fight.

1572—Sees supernova in Cassiopeia on November 11.

1573—Publishes book, *De stella nova*, about the supernova.

Kirsten Jørgensdatter becomes Tycho Brahe's *slegfred*, or common-law, wife.

Daughter Kirstine born.

1576—Given island of Hven by King Frederick II.

Construction of Uraniborg begins.

1577—Observes comet from November 13 to January 26, 1578.

1581—Uraniborg is ready. Kirsten and children move in.

1584—Construction of Stjerneborg, five underground observing chambers.

1587—Publishes *De mundi*, a detailed book about the comet of 1577.

1588—King Frederick II dies.

Denmark ruled by regency council of nobles.

1596—Christian IV crowned king of Denmark.

1597—Last observation at Uraniborg, March 15.

Leaves Hven, March 29.

Leaves Denmark, June 2.

1597—Receives letter and book from Johannes Kepler.

1599—Rudolph II, emperor of the Holy Roman Empire, becomes new patron.

Moves into Benatky Palace.

1600—Kepler arrives at Benatky.

1601—Moves to Prague at emperor's request.

Announces plan to develop tables of planetary movement with Kepler's help.

Dies October 24.

1604—Kirsten Brahe dies. Buried next to her husband in Prague's Teyn Cathedral.

1627—Johannes Kepler publishes *Rudolphine Tables*.

Chapter Notes

Chapter 1. The Castle of the Heavens

1. James S. Trefil, *Space, Time, Infinity: The Smithsonian Views the Universe* (New York: Pantheon, 1985), p. 38.

2. *Tycho Brahe's Description of His Instruments and Scientific Work as given in Astronomiae instauratae mechanica, Wandesburgi, 1598,* translated and edited by Hans Raeder, Elis Stromgren, and Bengt Stromgren (Kobenhavn: Det Kongelige Danske Videnskabernes Selskab, 1946), p. 110.

3. Ibid., p. 107.

Chapter 2. Noble Beginnings

1. Victor Thoren, *The Lord of Uraniborg: A Biography of Tycho Brahe* (New York: Cambridge University Press, 1990), p. 6.

2. John Robert Christianson, *On Tycho's Island: Tycho Brahe and His Assistants, 1570–1601* (New York: Cambridge University Press, 2000), p. 59.

3. Ibid., p. 12.

4. *Tycho Brahe's Description of His Instruments and Scientific Work as given in Astronomiae instauratae mechanica, Wandesburgi, 1598,* translated and edited by Hans Raeder, Elis Stromgren, and Bengt Stromgren (Kobenhavn: Det Kongelige Danske Videnskabernes Selskab, 1946), p. 106.

5. Victor Thoren, *The Lord of Uraniborg: A Biography of Tycho Brahe* (New York: Cambridge University Press, 1990), pp. 4–5.

6. *Tycho Brahe's Description of His Instruments and Scientific Work*, p. 106.

7. Thoren, p. 13.

8. J. L. E. Dreyer, *Tycho Brahe: A Picture of Scientific Life and Work in the Sixteenth Century* (New York: Dover Books, 1963), p. 14.

9. *Tycho Brahe's Description of his Instruments and Scientific Work*, p. 107.

10. Ibid.

Chapter 3. Jupiter, Saturn and Tycho's Nose

1. *Tycho Brahe's Description of His Instruments and Scientific Work as given in Astronomiae instauratae mechanica, Wandesburgi, 1598,* translated and edited by Hans Raeder, Elis Stromgren, and Bengt Stromgren (Kobenhavn: Det Kongelige Danske Videnskabernes Selskab, 1946), p. 107.

2. Ibid., p. 108.

3. Victor Thoren, *The Lord of Uraniborg: A Biography of Tycho Brahe* (New York: Cambridge University Press, 1990), p. 20.

4. Ibid., p. 22.

5. Ibid., pp. 25–26.

Chapter 4. Supernova!

1. Victor Thoren, *The Lord of Uraniborg: A Biography of Tycho Brahe* (New York: Cambridge University Press, 1990), p. 37.

2. J. L. E. Dreyer, *Tycho Brahe: A Picture of Scientific Life and Work in the Sixteenth Century* (New York: Dover Books, 1963), p. 38.

3. Ibid., p. 41.

4. Hartmut Frommert, "SN 1572, Tycho's Supernova," *Supernovae*, n.d., <www.seds.org/~spider/spider/Vars/sn1572.html> (June 12, 2001).

Chapter 5. Settling Down

1. John Robert Christianson, *On Tycho's Island: Tycho Brahe and His Assistants, 1570–1601* (New York: Cambridge University Press, 2000), p. 12.

2. Ibid., p. 13.

3. Ibid.

4. J. L. E. Dreyer, *Tycho Brahe: A Picture of Scientific Life and Work in the Sixteenth Century* (New York: Dover Books, 1963), p. 84.

5. *Tycho Brahe's Description of His Instruments and Scientific Work as given in Astronomiae instauratae mechanica, Wandesburgi, 1598*, translated and edited by Hans Raeder, Elis Stromgren, and Bengt Stromgren (Kobenhavn: Det Kongelige Danske Videnskabernes Selskab, 1946), p. 109.

6. Christianson, p. 29.

7. Ibid., p. 36.

Chapter 6. The Great Comet

1. John Robert Christianson, *On Tycho's Island: Tycho Brahe and His Assistants, 1570–1601* (New York: Cambridge University Press, 2000), p. 38.

2. Victor Thoren, *The Lord of Uraniborg: A Biography of Tycho Brahe* (New York: Cambridge University Press, 1990), p. 123.

3. Weldon Owen, *Reader's Digest Explores Astronomy* (Pleasantville, N.Y.: Reader's Digest Association, Inc., 1998), p. 105.

4. Charles Coulston Gillispie, *Dictionary of Scientific Biography* (New York: Scribner, 1970), vol. II, p. 407.

Chapter 7. Life at Uraniborg

1. *Tycho Brahe's Description of His Instruments and Scientific Work as given in Astronomiae instauratae mechanica, Wandesburgi, 1598*, translated and edited by Hans Raeder, Elis Stromgren, and Bengt Stromgren (Kobenhavn: Det Kongelige Danske Videnskabernes Selskab, 1946), p. 29.

2. John Robert Christianson, *On Tycho's Island: Tycho Brahe and his Assistants, 1570–1601* (New York: Cambridge University Press, 2000), p. 118.

3. Victor Thoren, *The Lord of Uraniborg: A Biography of Tycho Brahe* (New York: Cambridge University Press, 1990), p. 211.

4. Christianson, p. 277.

5. Ibid., pp. 313–314.

6. Ibid., p. 58.

7. Ibid., p. 77.

8. Ibid.

9. Ibid.

10. Ibid.

11. Ibid., p. 79.

12. Thoren, p. 322.

Chapter 8. Astronomy at Hven

1. *Tycho Brahe's Description of His Instruments and Scientific Work as given in Astronomiae instauratae mechanica, Wandesburgi, 1598*, translated and edited by Hans Raeder,

Elis Stromgren, and Bengt Stromgren (Kobenhavn: Det Kongelige Danske Videnskabernes Selskab, 1946), p. 109.

2. J. L. E. Dreyer, *Tycho Brahe: A Picture of Scientific Life and Work in the Sixteenth Century* (New York: Dover Books, 1963), p. 347.

3. Ibid., p. 178.

4. Charles Coulston Gillispie, *Dictionary of Scientific Biography* (New York: Scribner, 1970), vol. II, p. 411.

5. Dreyer, p. 334.

6. Victor Thoren, *The Lord of Uraniborg: A Biography of Tycho Brahe* (New York: Cambridge University Press, 1990), p. 190.

7. Weldon Owen, *Reader's Digest Explores Astronomy* (Pleasantville, N.Y.: Reader's Digest Association, Inc., 1998), p. 105.

Chapter 9. Leaving Denmark

1. J. L. E. Dreyer, *Tycho Brahe: A Picture of Scientific Life and Work in the Sixteenth Century* (New York: Dover Books, 1963), p. 108.

2. Ibid., p. 110.

3. Ibid., p. 153.

4. John Robert Christianson, *On Tycho's Island: Tycho Brahe and His Assistants, 1570–1601* (New York: Cambridge University Press, 2000), p. 110.

5. Victor Thoren, *The Lord of Uraniborg: A Biography of Tycho Brahe* (New York: Cambridge University Press, 1990), p. 343.

6. Christianson, p. 185.

7. Ibid., p. 167.

8. Ibid., p. 202.

Chapter 10. Exile

1. John Robert Christianson, *On Tycho's Island: Tycho Brahe and his Assistants, 1570–1601* (New York: Cambridge University Press, 2000), p. 209.

2. Ibid., p. 213.

3. J. L. E. Dreyer, *Tycho Brahe: A Picture of Scientific Life and Work in the Sixteenth Century* (New York: Dover Books, 1963), p. 265.

4. Charles Coulston Gillispie, *Dictionary of Scientific Biography* (New York: Scribner, 1970), vol. VII, p. 291.

5. Victor Thoren, *The Lord of Uraniborg: A Biography of Tycho Brahe* (New York: Cambridge University Press, 1990), p. 412.

6. Ibid., p. 433.

7. *Landskrona Cultur Department*, n.d., <www.landskrona.se/kultur/engelsk/index.html> (June 12, 2001).

Chapter 11. Tycho Brahe's Legacy

1. J. L. E. Dreyer, *Tycho Brahe: A Picture of Scientific Life and Work in the Sixteenth Century* (New York: Dover Books, 1963), p. 376.

2. John Robert Christianson, *On Tycho's Island: Tycho Brahe and His Assistants, 1570–1601* (New York: Cambridge University Press, 2000), p. 248.

3. Petr Hadrava, "Preface to Mechanica by Tycho Brahe," n.d., <http://sunkl.asu.cas.cz/~had/tychpref.html> (June 12, 2001).

Glossary

alchemy—An early form of chemistry. Alchemists often experimented to change one substance into another. Some alchemists believed they could change common metals into gold. In Tycho Brahe's time, alchemy also dealt with medicine and healing.

altitude—The elevation of a celestial object above the horizon measured in degrees.

astronomical radius—An instrument used to measure the angle between celestial objects.

astronomy—The science of the celestial bodies; the study of the origins, motion, and composition, of the stars, planets, comets, and other bodies.

astrology—The study of the supposed influence of heavenly bodies on happenings on Earth.

celestial—Of the heavens or sky or universe. Celestial bodies include planets, comets, asteroids, and stars.

celestial Globe—A globe on which the stars and constellations are shown.

celestial Sphere—The imaginary sphere that surrounds Earth upon which the celestial objects appear to be positioned.

comet—A small celestial body made of ice, dust, and gas and usually having a tail.

conjunction—The apparent meeting or passing of two or more celestial bodies.

constellation—One of the eighty-eight identified patterns of stars.

eclipse—The effect when one celestial body passes into the shadow of another. In a lunar eclipse, Earth's shadow falls on the moon. In a solar eclipse, the moon passes between Earth and the sun.

ellipse—An oval shape. The orbits of the planets and comets around the sun are ellipses.

fief—Land and its tenants granted by a king to a noble to oversee in exchange for service.

mural—A large painting on a wall.

opposition—The position of two celestial bodies in which one is exactly opposite the other on the celestial sphere. Usually an opposition of the sun and a planet.

orbit—The path followed by an object in space around a more massive object.

parallax—The shift in an object's position when seen from two different points.

Pegasus—A flying horse in Greek mythology who flew to the heavens.

quadrant—An instrument shaped like a quarter circle, used for measuring angles and heights.

sextant—An instrument shaped like one-sixth of a circle, used for measuring angles and heights.

slegfred—A Danish common-law wife.

supernova—A huge star that brilliantly explodes at the end of its life.

Further Reading

Andronik, Catherine M. *Copernicus: Founder of Modern Astronomy*. Berkeley Heights, N.J.: Enslow Publishers, Inc., 2002.

Bonar, Samantha. *Comets*. New York: Franklin Watts, 1998.

MacDonald, Fiona. *Space*. Danbury, Conn.: Franklin Watts, Inc., 2000.

Segal, Justin. *The Amazing Space Almanac*. Los Angeles: Lowell House Juvenile, 1999.

Snowden, S. *The Young Astronomer*. Tulsa, Okla.: E D C Publishing, 1999.

Internet Addresses

Tycho Brahe Official Website
http://www.tychobrahe.com

Hven, the island in Oresund
http://www.hven.com/INDEXE.html

The Noble Dane: Images of Tycho Brahe
http://www.mhs.ox.ac.uk/tycho/index.htm

Tycho Brahe, Danish Astronomer
http://www.nada.kth.se/~fred/tycho.html

Index